MAYER SMITH

A Heart of Silver and Ash

Copyright © 2025 by Mayer Smith

All rights reserved. No part of this publication may be reproduced, stored or transmitted in any form or by any means, electronic, mechanical, photocopying, recording, scanning, or otherwise without written permission from the publisher. It is illegal to copy this book, post it to a website, or distribute it by any other means without permission.

This novel is entirely a work of fiction. The names, characters and incidents portrayed in it are the work of the author's imagination. Any resemblance to actual persons, living or dead, events or localities is entirely coincidental.

Mayer Smith asserts the moral right to be identified as the author of this work.

Mayer Smith has no responsibility for the persistence or accuracy of URLs for external or third-party Internet Websites referred to in this publication and does not guarantee that any content on such Websites is, or will remain, accurate or appropriate.

Designations used by companies to distinguish their products are often claimed as trademarks. All brand names and product names used in this book and on its cover are trade names, service marks, trademarks and registered trademarks of their respective owners. The publishers and the book are not associated with any product or vendor mentioned in this book. None of the companies referenced within the book have endorsed the book.

First edition

This book was professionally typeset on Reedsy.
Find out more at reedsy.com

Contents

1	The Silver Locket	1
2	Whispers in the Dark	7
3	The Forgotten Path	14
4	The Silver Mark	21
5	The Unseen Enemy	27
6	The Ashen Encounter	34
7	The Choice of Silver and Ash	41
8	Heart in the Flames	47
9	The Ritual of Blood and Ash	54
10	The Heart of the Storm	60
11	Into the Ashes	67
12	Heart Reborn	73

One

The Silver Locket

E velyn's fingers trembled as she held the letter, the paper worn and creased at the edges, the ink faded yet still legible. It was a letter she had never expected to see again—its contents a ghost from a life she had long buried. A life she had long tried to forget. The letter had arrived that morning, tucked under the door of her modest apartment with no return address, just her name written in elegant script.

Her breath hitched as she read the first few words. "Find me, before the ashes consume us both."

The handwriting was unmistakable. Arden's.

It had been seven years since he vanished without a trace, leaving only silence in his wake. The unanswered questions, the painful goodbyes, all had become nothing more than a distant ache, buried deep beneath layers of time. But now, this. This letter. This promise. A thread pulling her back into a past she had worked so hard to escape.

The letter smelled faintly of cedarwood—an earthy, comforting scent that she immediately associated with him. Arden had always worn the same cologne. The smell brought a flood of memories, both sweet and bitter. She had loved him once, with all the fire of a first love, but something had changed. Something had driven them apart. She had tried to let go, tried to forget the way his touch had felt, the way his smile had made her heart race, but now—now she found herself standing on the precipice of that old life, just as torn as she had been all those years ago.

Evelyn's pulse quickened as she read the last line again, as if her eyes were trying to piece together something that made sense, but it didn't. "Find me, before the ashes consume us both."

Her hand clenched around the letter as if holding it would keep her from shattering into a million pieces. She had to know what it meant. She had to know where he was.

The world outside her apartment window was grey, the overcast sky threatening rain. The bustling streets of the city, usually filled with noise and life, felt muffled from the inside. She stared at the letter for a long moment, the words burning into her mind. She couldn't stay here. She couldn't let this go unanswered.

She shoved the letter into her coat pocket, her decision already made, but as she moved toward the door, a knock stopped her.

It was a soft knock—just one tap—but it felt like a warning, like something was about to shift in the air. Evelyn hesitated, her heart skipping a beat as she slowly approached the door. Who could it be? A delivery? A neighbor? Or someone from her past?

With a steadying breath, she opened the door, and there he stood.

Sebastian.

His dark eyes met hers, and for a moment, neither of them spoke. He looked exactly the same—tall, broad-shouldered, with the same intensity in his gaze. His raven-black hair was slightly longer than it had been the last time she saw him, falling over his brow in messy waves, but everything else about him was unchanged. The way he stood, the way his jaw clenched when he was frustrated, the way his lips barely curled into a smile.

"Evelyn," he said, his voice deep and rough with something unsaid. He shifted his weight, looking at her as if he had expected her to be someone else—someone she wasn't anymore.

"Sebastian." Her voice came out breathless, and she quickly looked away, as if the very sound of his name could burn her.

"I didn't think I'd find you here," he continued, glancing down at the letter she was still holding. "I had no idea you were still living in the city."

Evelyn tried to mask her surprise. She had thought he was long gone, moved on to wherever life had led him after they had parted ways. She didn't want to think about their shared history, the way they had once been inseparable, before it all fell apart. Before Arden had come into the picture.

"I could ask you the same thing," Evelyn replied, her voice steady, though her heart raced in her chest. "What are you doing here, Sebastian?"

He didn't immediately answer, his gaze flickering to the letter again, and then back to her. The tension between them was palpable, and Evelyn could feel it pressing down on her chest, making it hard to breathe. There had always been something between them—something complicated, something unspoken. He had always known her better than anyone else. Perhaps that was why he had walked away when Arden had come into her life.

"I should have come sooner," he said finally, his tone softer, though still guarded. "But I had to know if you'd ever truly let him go."

Her heart skipped. "What do you mean?"

Sebastian's eyes darkened, a flicker of something dangerous passing through them. "The letter. You're looking for him, aren't you?"

Evelyn's breath caught in her throat. "How did you know about the letter?"

"I know you," he said simply. "I know how you think. How you always think you can save people. You can't save him, Evelyn."

The words stung more than she expected, but she stood her ground. "I have to try. I need to know what happened. Why he left. Why he—"

"Why he disappeared? Why he's been gone for so long?" Sebastian interrupted, his voice rising with a bitterness she hadn't expected. "You really think you'll find answers? You think it'll make a difference? Arden's gone. He's gone, and you need to move on."

The finality in his voice struck her like a slap. She had never imagined hearing those words from him. Of all the people in her life, Sebastian had always been the one who understood her the most. But now, there was a distance between them—an unspoken wall she couldn't tear down.

"I don't believe that," she said quietly, her gaze fixed on his. "I think Arden's still out there. And I think he's in danger."

Sebastian took a step closer, his presence overwhelming. "You're wrong. Whatever you think you're going to find, it's not going to be the truth. You're looking for a ghost."

But Evelyn didn't believe him. Arden wasn't a ghost. He was out there, and she would find him. She had to. For herself. For the man she once loved.

The silence that followed hung thick, oppressive. Then, with a final glance at the letter, Sebastian stepped back. "You're making a mistake, Evelyn," he warned, his voice low. "Don't follow this path."

But Evelyn was already moving toward the door, the weight of the letter still pressing heavily in her pocket. "I have to," she whispered, more to herself than to him.

Sebastian's expression flickered with something unreadable before he turned and walked away, disappearing into the hallway. The door clicked shut behind him, but the echo of his warning still lingered in the air.

Evelyn's heart raced as she picked up the silver locket from the table, the locket she had found earlier that morning, just before the letter arrived. It had been left behind by Arden. A relic of their past. She could almost hear his voice in her mind, soft and urgent. Find me.

She had no idea what dangers lay ahead, what secrets would be unearthed, but she couldn't turn back now. There was no choice.

And so, Evelyn set out into the world, her heart a tangle of hope and fear, chasing the shadows of a love that had never truly died.

Two

Whispers in the Dark

The manor was as she remembered it—silent, old, and heavy with the scent of aged wood and dust. Evelyn stood on the threshold, her hand gripping the brass doorknob as if it might break under her touch. She hadn't been back in years. Not since the day Arden left. Not since everything had shattered into a thousand jagged pieces.

The letter had led her here. The silver locket, the cryptic words, all of it pointed to this forgotten place—her family's estate, now a crumbling relic of a past better left buried. But something about it called to her, pulling her deeper into a mystery that was as much about her as it was about Arden.

Her breath caught in her throat as the door creaked open, the hinges protesting after years of disuse. The first thing that hit her was the cold. A chill that sank into her bones, curling around her like the hands of a ghost. The air tasted stale, heavy with the scent of decay, of time holding its breath.

The grand foyer stretched out before her, the marble floors cracked and yellowed with age. A grand chandelier hung above, its crystals dull, the light from the hallway outside failing to pierce the darkness of the room. Her heels clicked sharply against the floor as she stepped inside, the sound echoing unnervingly in the vast emptiness.

Evelyn's pulse quickened as she took in the familiar surroundings—the faded tapestries on the walls, the broken furniture draped in white sheets, and the long staircase that spiraled upward into the unknown. Everything seemed frozen in time, as if the manor had been waiting for her return, but for what purpose, she could not say.

She closed her eyes for a moment, the memories rushing at her like a flood. She had grown up here, among the grand halls and the winding staircases, playing hide-and-seek in the labyrinth of rooms. But all those memories were now tainted with the presence of Arden, his dark eyes, his haunting smile, and the love they had shared.

Her heart clenched at the thought of him—of everything they had lost. But the letter, the promise… it was enough to pull her forward, to silence the fear gnawing at the edges of her resolve.

With a deep breath, she moved past the foyer and into the main hall. The shadows clung to the walls, stretching long and dark as the light from the door behind her dimmed. Every step she took seemed to stir the air, and the silence was deafening. As if the house itself were holding its breath, waiting.

She made her way to the study, where she remembered Arden spending hours poring over books and scribbling in his journals. He had always been so secretive about those journals. He'd said they were for his eyes only, that the things written within them were too dangerous to be shared. Yet, Evelyn had always been curious. Now, she wished she had asked him more. Wished she had demanded to know what he was hiding.

The door to the study stood ajar, a faint light spilling out from within. Evelyn hesitated for a moment, then pushed it open, the sound of the wood scraping against the frame making her skin prickle.

The room was just as it had been all those years ago, the shelves lined with dusty books, the worn leather chair by the window where Arden used to sit. But now, there was an eerie stillness, the air heavy with the weight of forgotten things. The window was slightly cracked, and a soft breeze stirred the drapes, sending a shiver down her spine.

Her eyes darted to the desk, where a single journal sat in the middle of the cluttered surface. The cover was old, the leather cracked and faded, but the gold initials on the front gleamed in the dim light. A.B.

Arden's journal.

Her heart skipped a beat. She stepped forward, her fingers

brushing over the worn surface. The temptation to open it was overwhelming, but she resisted for a moment. She needed to be sure. She needed to know what she was walking into. The answers she sought might be within these pages, but so might the things she wasn't ready to face.

Just as her hand closed around the journal, a noise echoed through the manor, sharp and sudden. A low creak, like the sound of a door opening somewhere deep within the house. Evelyn froze, her breath catching in her throat. The sound was soft, almost imperceptible, but it made her pulse race, as if something—or someone—was lurking just beyond her reach.

Her instincts kicked in, and she dropped the journal back onto the desk, her heart pounding in her ears. There was no reason for anyone to be here, not unless they were expecting her.

She stepped back toward the door, her footsteps silent against the creaking floorboards. The sound of the door opening had been faint, but there was no mistaking it. Someone was in the house.

Her fingers instinctively brushed the locket tucked into her pocket, the cool metal against her skin grounding her. She hadn't noticed it before, but now, it felt heavier than it had when she first picked it up. It was as though it were urging her to move, to follow the path that had been set before her.

The hairs on the back of her neck prickled as she slowly opened the door and slipped out into the hallway, her breath shallow and quick. The light from the study barely reached the dark corners of the corridor, and the silence that followed was suffocating.

She could feel the presence now—someone was watching her. She wasn't alone.

The door at the end of the hall creaked open, the faintest hint of light spilling from the crack. Evelyn's heart raced as she approached, her body tense, every muscle in her body coiled with anticipation. She had no idea what lay beyond that door, but she knew she had to find out.

As she reached for the doorknob, she caught a glimpse of movement in the shadows. A figure, just out of sight. She couldn't make out the face, but there was something familiar about the posture, the way they moved. It was as if they had been waiting for her all along.

Before she could react, the door swung open, revealing a room she didn't recognize. The walls were lined with shelves, filled with old books and strange artifacts. The air inside was thick with the smell of incense, and the faint hum of something ancient lingered in the atmosphere.

And there, in the center of the room, stood a man.

He was tall, with dark hair that fell messily over his forehead, and his eyes, cold and calculating, locked onto hers with an intensity that made her stomach churn. He was no stranger to her.

"Sebastian," she whispered, the word slipping from her lips before she could stop it.

He smirked, a slow, almost predatory smile that sent a shiver down her spine. "Did you really think you could find the answers you're looking for so easily, Evelyn?"

Evelyn's breath caught in her throat. "What are you doing here?"

"I think you already know," he said, stepping forward, his presence filling the room. "You've always been curious. You always wanted to uncover the truth, no matter what it cost you."

Her heart hammered in her chest as she tried to read him, to figure out what he was playing at. There was something in his eyes, something that told her this wasn't just a coincidence. Sebastian knew more about Arden's disappearance than he was letting on, and he was hiding something—something dangerous.

"Where is he?" she demanded, stepping forward, her voice trembling with a mix of fear and determination. "What do you know about Arden?"

Sebastian's smile faded, his expression turning colder. "You really want to know? The truth isn't something you can just walk into, Evelyn. It's not something you can undo once you've opened the door."

He was right. She could feel it in the very marrow of her bones—the weight of the truth pressing down on her. She had come this far. She couldn't turn back now.

"I don't care what it costs," Evelyn whispered, her voice steady despite the storm raging inside her. "I need to know what happened to him."

Sebastian's eyes narrowed, and for a fleeting moment, she saw something like pity in them. "Then you're already too late," he said softly. "The ashes are already here."

Three

The Forgotten Path

The winding path ahead was shrouded in darkness, the trees above twisting like gnarled fingers reaching out to grasp at the air. Evelyn could hear the distant rustling of leaves in the wind, but the forest around her was otherwise silent, a heavy stillness hanging in the air as though even the birds dared not sing. She had always loved the woods surrounding her family's estate, but tonight, the familiar trees felt menacing—alive with secrets, hiding shadows that seemed to watch her every move.

Her footsteps were quiet against the soft earth, but even in the silence, every crack of a twig underfoot sounded too loud, as if the forest itself was listening. She felt a chill that had little to do with the night air creeping under her skin, a gnawing sense that something was waiting, something she hadn't yet understood.

The Forgotten Path

She had left the manor hours ago, her heart racing with a mix of determination and dread as she followed the path outlined in Arden's last letter. The words on that paper had burned themselves into her mind, urging her onward. Find me, before the ashes consume us both. It was cryptic, laden with meaning she couldn't quite grasp, but Evelyn knew one thing for sure: Arden was alive, somewhere in these woods.

The silver locket pressed against her chest, its cold metal a constant reminder of the past she couldn't escape. It was the only clue she had left, the only tether to the man she had loved so fiercely—and still loved, despite the years that had passed. She had to find him. She had to understand what he had become.

Her breath caught in her throat as the wind shifted, sending a flurry of leaves scattering across the path. For a brief moment, she thought she saw something—someone—moving in the distance. A shadow, just beyond the reach of the moonlight. Her heart leapt in her chest, and her pulse quickened.

"Arden?" she whispered, her voice barely more than a breath, carried away by the wind.

No answer. Just the rustling of the trees and the oppressive silence that followed. She swallowed hard, shaking off the fear that tried to tighten its grip on her. It could have been an animal, a figment of her imagination. Or it could have been someone else entirely.

The path twisted further into the woods, disappearing into the underbrush, but she pressed on, each step taking her deeper into the darkness. The air grew heavier, thick with moisture and the scent of wet earth, and the trees seemed to close in around her, their branches like fingers brushing against her skin.

Minutes—or perhaps hours—passed as she walked, her thoughts a blur, consumed by the need to find him. The deeper she went, the more she felt the presence of something unseen, something watching her from the shadows. Every rustle of the leaves, every snap of a twig beneath her feet, felt as if it were leading her somewhere, pulling her closer to a truth she wasn't sure she was ready for.

Then, just as she thought she might turn back, the path opened into a clearing. The moonlight bathed the area in pale light, casting long shadows across the ground. The trees here were thinner, their trunks standing tall and straight like sentinels guarding something hidden.

In the center of the clearing stood an ancient stone well, its edges worn smooth by time, moss creeping up its sides, thick and green in the dim light. The air here felt different, as if the very earth was holding its breath. Evelyn stepped forward, drawn by the pull of something ancient, something familiar.

As her hand brushed against the stone, the hairs on the back of her neck stood up. She wasn't alone.

A voice, low and urgent, broke the stillness. "You shouldn't be here."

Evelyn froze, her heart leaping into her throat. The voice was unmistakable. It was him—Arden.

"Arden?" she called out, her voice trembling. She scanned the clearing, but there was no sign of him. The moonlight revealed only the well, the trees, and the silent stretch of earth beneath her feet. "Where are you?"

A rustle to her right. She spun around, her breath catching in her chest. From the darkness, a figure emerged—a tall, shadowy shape that stepped into the light. Arden.

Her pulse quickened at the sight of him, the man she had loved, standing before her as though he had never left. He was thinner, his face gaunt, his eyes dark and heavy with something unspoken. His clothes were torn, stained with dirt, but there was no mistaking him.

"Evelyn…" His voice was strained, as though the very act of speaking took something out of him. "You shouldn't have come."

She took a step forward, her heart pounding in her chest, her eyes locked onto him. "Arden, what's happened? Where have you been? Why did you leave me?" Her words tumbled out in a rush, the questions she had carried for years finally spilling from her lips.

He shook his head, stepping back as if he couldn't bear to be near her. "I never wanted to hurt you," he said, his voice barely above a whisper. "But you don't understand. You have to leave.

It's too dangerous for you."

Evelyn's breath caught in her throat. "What's going on, Arden? You've been gone for so long, and now you show up, looking like—" She stopped herself, her mind racing, trying to make sense of the man standing before her. He was here, but he wasn't the same. Something had changed. Something was wrong.

His eyes darkened, and he took another step back, as if the distance between them was something he needed. "You don't know what I've become," he said, his voice cracking. "I'm not the man you once knew, Evelyn. I'm… I'm something else now."

Her heart broke at the pain in his voice, at the way his words echoed with the weight of untold secrets. But there was no turning back now. She had come too far.

"I don't care what you've become," she said, stepping forward, ignoring the rising panic in her chest. "I just want to know what happened. I need to understand."

Arden's gaze flickered to the ground, his jaw tightening. "You can't help me," he murmured, his voice heavy with regret. "I've made a deal with forces I can't control. It's already too late for me. But not for you. You can still walk away."

The tension in the air was suffocating. Every word, every glance, seemed to carry a weight that threatened to crush her. But Evelyn wouldn't back down. She couldn't. She had already made the choice when she followed him here.

"I won't leave you," she said firmly, her voice steady despite the fear clawing at her. "Whatever you've become, I'll stay with you. We'll find a way through this together."

Arden looked at her for a long moment, his eyes searching hers, as though trying to find the resolve he once knew in her. But the hesitation in his eyes was clear. He didn't believe her. He didn't believe there was a way out. And maybe he was right. Maybe the forces that had claimed him were too powerful, too ancient to fight. But Evelyn refused to believe it.

She stepped closer, her heart pounding in her chest, and reached for his hand. He flinched, his body stiffening as if her touch pained him. But she held on, her grip firm and resolute.

"Arden," she whispered, her voice trembling with a mixture of desperation and hope. "I won't give up on you."

For a moment, there was only silence between them, the distant sound of the wind moving through the trees the only sound in the night. And then, finally, Arden's shoulders slumped, his gaze softening as he met her eyes.

"You shouldn't have come, Evelyn," he whispered again, but this time, there was no bitterness in his voice. Only a quiet sorrow. "But now that you're here… we'll see it through. Together."

But even as he spoke the words, the shadows around them seemed to close in, darker and more threatening than before. And Evelyn couldn't shake the feeling that they were being watched by something far older, far darker than either of them could comprehend.

Four

The Silver Mark

The moon hung low in the sky, casting an eerie silver glow over the clearing as Evelyn stood with Arden, the silence between them heavy, oppressive. The forest around them whispered with life, but neither of them moved, as if they were both waiting for something to break the stillness. The only sound was the wind, rustling the leaves in the trees, the faintest hum of something ancient that seemed to vibrate through the ground beneath their feet.

Evelyn's heart was pounding in her chest, her breath shallow. Arden stood before her, his body taut with tension, his eyes dark and distant, like a man lost in a world of his own making. She could see the subtle tremble in his hands as he reached up to tug the sleeve of his worn jacket, pulling it back to reveal the skin of his forearm.

Her breath hitched in her throat as she saw it—the silver mark, etched into his flesh. It was a strange, intricate symbol, something she'd never seen before, like a twisted design of flowing lines that seemed to move when she looked at them too closely. The mark gleamed faintly under the moonlight, a stark contrast to the pale skin of his arm.

"What is it?" she asked, her voice barely a whisper, her eyes locked on the mark.

Arden's jaw tightened, and he quickly pulled his sleeve back down, as though the mark itself was a thing too dangerous to be seen. But Evelyn had already seen it, and she couldn't unsee it. She needed to know more.

"I didn't want you to know about this," Arden murmured, his voice thick with regret. "It's not something anyone should know about."

Evelyn reached out instinctively, her fingers trembling as they brushed against his arm, her touch gentle but firm. "You can't keep this from me," she said, her voice trembling with emotion. "Whatever it is, it's tied to you. To everything that's happening."

Arden's eyes flickered with something unreadable, a mixture of fear and something darker, something she couldn't quite place. He stepped back, his body tense as if preparing to flee, but Evelyn refused to let him pull away.

"Please, Arden," she whispered, stepping closer, her breath catching in her throat. "Tell me what it means."

For a long moment, Arden said nothing. The wind rustled through the trees again, the sound both calming and unnerving. Finally, he spoke, his voice low and strained.

"The mark is... it's part of a curse," he said slowly, his words heavy with a weight Evelyn couldn't begin to comprehend. "It's what keeps me alive. And it's what's slowly killing me."

Evelyn's breath caught in her chest, and she stepped back, her mind reeling. "A curse? What kind of curse?"

Arden's eyes closed briefly, his hand coming up to his forehead as though trying to push away the thoughts that were tormenting him. He looked exhausted, as if the weight of everything was too much to bear.

"It's not just any curse," he said finally, his voice rough. "It's ancient. And it's tied to my bloodline. My family, my ancestors—they made a pact with something... something that's not entirely human."

Evelyn could feel the air around her grow heavier, charged with an energy she couldn't explain. Her heart raced, but she couldn't look away from Arden's face, from the torment in his eyes. She had to know more. She had to understand what he was saying, even if it meant venturing into a world she wasn't sure she was ready for.

"Tell me," she whispered. "Tell me what happened. What did your family do?"

Arden's gaze flickered to the ground, his eyes dark with shame. He seemed to wrestle with the words, as though speaking them out loud would make the reality of it all too real.

"They made a bargain," he said, his voice barely audible. "They thought they could control it—control what they were dealing with. But they couldn't. It got out of hand. The curse…it spreads, and it only gets worse with each generation."

A shiver ran down Evelyn's spine as she absorbed his words. The curse had spread. Arden was part of it, but so was his bloodline. And now, she was standing in the middle of it, drawn into something far darker than she had ever imagined.

"Is that why you left?" she asked, her voice barely above a whisper. "Because of this curse? Because of what you've become?"

Arden didn't answer right away, his gaze distant as he stared at the ground, his jaw clenched. Then, finally, he looked up, his eyes meeting hers. They were full of something—something like desperation, like a man who had given up, who had already accepted his fate.

"I left because I thought I could protect you," he said quietly. "I thought I could keep you safe from this—this thing that's eating me alive. But it's already too late. I've already made the deal. I've already become part of it. And there's no going back."

The words hit Evelyn like a blow to the chest. The weight of his confession was overwhelming, suffocating. She could see the pain in his eyes, the resignation in the way he held himself, but it wasn't enough. It couldn't be enough.

"No," she said, her voice trembling with emotion. "You're wrong. It's never too late."

Arden looked at her as though she had spoken a foreign language, his expression unreadable. "You don't understand," he murmured. "You don't know what I've done. The things I've seen. The things I've had to sacrifice."

"I don't care," she said, her voice firmer now. "I don't care what you've done. I care about you. And I'm not leaving you like this."

For a moment, Arden didn't speak, his eyes flickering with something like disbelief, then something softer, something deeper. She could see the conflict in him, the struggle between the man he had been and the man he had become. It was there, in the way his shoulders slumped, in the way his chest heaved as if the weight of everything was too much to bear.

But then, slowly, almost hesitantly, he reached out, his hand trembling as it found hers. The contact sent a jolt of warmth through her, the connection between them so immediate, so electric, that it made her heart flutter in her chest.

"I'm sorry," he whispered, his voice breaking as his thumb brushed over the back of her hand. "I never wanted this for you. I never wanted to drag you into this."

Evelyn's heart ached as she looked into his eyes, as she saw the raw vulnerability in him, the man who had once been so certain, so unshakeable, now crumbling under the weight of his own curse. She couldn't let him go. Not now. Not when she was so close to understanding the truth.

"I'm not leaving you," she said, her voice resolute. "We'll find a way out of this. Together."

Arden's eyes searched hers for a long moment, and then, as if he had made a decision, he nodded. Slowly, almost imperceptibly, the weight of the moment lifted, and for the first time in what felt like an eternity, there was a flicker of hope in his gaze.

But the silence between them was heavy, like the calm before the storm. They both knew that the path ahead would be fraught with danger, and yet, in that moment, they stood together, bound by something neither of them could escape—the silver mark, the curse, and a love that neither time nor fate could sever.

And Evelyn knew, deep down, that this was only the beginning.

Five

The Unseen Enemy

The moon had disappeared behind a heavy cloud, leaving the forest draped in darkness as thick as velvet. Evelyn's breath was sharp in her chest, the cold air biting her skin as she walked beside Arden, her every step falling in sync with his. Their footsteps were muffled by the thick undergrowth, but the silence of the woods made even the smallest sound seem amplified. The crunch of leaves underfoot, the occasional rustle of the trees, the flutter of wings overhead— all seemed to carry a warning. The oppressive weight of the night pressed in around them, and Evelyn couldn't shake the feeling that they were being watched.

Arden's profile was dark against the shadowed landscape, his features sharp in the dim light, his movements tense. He hadn't said much since they left the clearing, his silence a heavy weight between them. Evelyn knew he was lost in his thoughts, struggling with the curse that had bound him in ways she couldn't fully understand. But even though he was right beside her, there was an invisible distance that seemed to stretch between them, a distance that felt like an insurmountable divide.

She wanted to reach out, to close the gap between them, but every time she tried, he pulled away. His gaze was distant, as if his mind was elsewhere, tangled in the past or lost in whatever darkness had claimed him.

"Arden," she said softly, her voice breaking the silence between them. "What do we do now?"

He didn't answer immediately. His jaw tightened, and his eyes flickered briefly in her direction before they returned to the path ahead. "We keep moving," he said, his voice rough, as though it cost him something to speak. "There's nothing else we can do."

The words stung, but Evelyn nodded, her pulse quickening as the sense of unease grew stronger. The forest around them had become unnervingly quiet. Too quiet. It was as though the very world had held its breath, waiting. The path they followed had grown narrow, winding between trees that seemed to close in around them, their trunks twisted and dark. There were no more signs of life—no birds, no animals rustling in the underbrush. It was as if all the creatures of the forest had vanished.

The air grew thick, heavy with something she couldn't quite

name. There was an unfamiliar tension in the atmosphere, a low hum that seemed to vibrate through the ground, sending a ripple of fear through her veins. The only sound now was the beat of her heart, pulsing in her ears, and the soft swish of their clothing as they moved.

"Something's not right," Evelyn murmured, glancing at Arden. His expression had darkened, his eyes scanning the shadows around them, alert but unreadable.

"I know," he said, his voice low. He stopped suddenly, his gaze locking onto the darkness ahead. "There's someone else here."

Evelyn's breath caught in her throat, her heart thudding painfully in her chest. "What do you mean? Who?"

Arden's eyes narrowed, his hand instinctively moving to the hilt of a knife that hung at his side. "I'm not sure. But they've been following us for hours."

Evelyn's skin prickled, the hairs on the back of her neck standing up. She turned slowly, scanning the shadows, but there was nothing. The trees stood still, their dark silhouettes looming like silent watchers. There was no sign of movement, no trace of life. But she could feel it. The presence. Like an invisible weight pressing against her chest, suffocating her.

"Why didn't you say something earlier?" she asked, her voice sharp with the sudden rush of fear.

"I didn't want to alarm you," Arden replied, his voice flat, though she could hear the tension in it. "But we need to keep moving. If they're here, they're not alone."

Before she could respond, a sound pierced the air—a low, guttural growl from somewhere in the darkness. Evelyn froze, her blood running cold. It was close. Too close.

Arden's body went rigid, and without a word, he grabbed her arm and pulled her off the path, dragging her into the cover of the trees. She barely had time to react, her heart pounding in her ears as she stumbled after him. The brush around them crackled as they pushed through it, their footsteps muffled by the thick underbrush. Arden's grip on her wrist was firm, guiding her with an urgency that spoke of danger—real danger.

They crouched behind a large, gnarled tree, the roots twisting up from the ground like jagged fingers. Evelyn's breath was shallow, her eyes darting between the darkness and Arden's tense form. She could hear the low growls again, closer this time, the sound vibrating through her chest. She couldn't see anything, but she knew something was out there. Something that wasn't human.

Arden's eyes flicked to her, his gaze dark with something that could have been fear—or something darker. His jaw clenched, and he pulled her closer, hiding them further in the shadows. "Stay quiet," he whispered, his voice a low command.

Evelyn nodded, her pulse racing, but she couldn't tear her gaze away from the shadows, her mind working to process everything she had learned. Who were they? What was out there? And why was Arden so determined to protect her? She hadn't thought about it before, but now, the answer was painfully clear: whatever was following them was part of the curse. Part of the reason Arden had disappeared.

The growls grew louder, more distinct. Evelyn's breath caught as a shape moved through the darkness, just beyond the reach of the trees. She couldn't make out the figure, but it was large—too large. And its movements were unnatural, as if it were something that didn't belong in the world they knew.

Her eyes widened as another shape appeared beside it, and then another. They were closing in, surrounding them.

Arden's grip tightened on her wrist, his body tense, his breath steady but controlled. He didn't look at her, didn't speak, but she could feel the weight of his thoughts pressing down on her. His face was set in grim determination, the same expression he had worn when they had first entered the woods—when he had known something was wrong, but hadn't said anything.

There was a crack from behind them, a twig snapping underfoot. The sound was small, insignificant to anyone else, but to Evelyn, it was a warning.

Arden's hand shot out, pulling her further into the shadows. "Stay down," he hissed, his voice urgent.

Evelyn barely had time to react before a figure stepped into the clearing, its tall, shadowy form gliding silently between the trees. It moved with the grace of a predator—its eyes glowing faintly, reflecting the moonlight in a way that sent a shiver down her spine. She couldn't make out its face, couldn't see anything but its silhouette, but she could feel its presence, looming over them.

Arden's grip on her wrist was the only thing keeping her grounded. He was breathing through his teeth, his muscles coiled, ready to spring into action at any moment.

And then, the figure spoke, its voice a low, guttural growl that made Evelyn's stomach churn.

"It's time," it said, its tone cold and menacing. "Time to collect what's ours."

Evelyn's pulse spiked, her mind racing. She didn't understand what it meant, but she could feel the danger thickening around them. The words hung in the air like a threat, and she knew—deep down—that whatever this was, it wasn't just following them. It had been sent for them. Sent for Arden.

Before she could respond, the figure stepped forward, and another shape emerged from the shadows. There was no way out now. They were surrounded.

Arden's voice, barely a whisper, filled her ear. "Don't make a sound," he warned. "They're here for me, but they'll take you too, if you get in their way."

Evelyn's breath faltered. Her heart raced with terror, but her gaze never wavered from the figures in the darkness. This was only the beginning. And whatever this was, she couldn't let it tear them apart.

Six

The Ashen Encounter

The darkness was suffocating, the night air thick with an unnatural chill that seeped into Evelyn's bones. She barely felt the cold anymore, her senses numb to the sharp bite of the wind, her heart pounding in her chest. The figures that surrounded them—silent and deadly—had moved closer, their presence an overwhelming weight in the space between the trees. She could hear their breathing now, slow and measured, like a predator's breath before the strike.

Arden's grip tightened on her wrist, pulling her deeper into the shadows of the towering trees, his eyes flicking back and forth, scanning their surroundings with a predator's precision. She could feel the tension in his body, his muscles coiled, ready to spring into action, yet he held himself still, every movement controlled, every breath quiet. But despite his composure, Evelyn could sense the fear that radiated off him—subtle, but

The Ashen Encounter

undeniable.

"We're not alone," Arden murmured, his voice barely above a whisper, though the words still seemed to echo in her mind, heavy and foreboding. "There's something else here. Something worse than what you've seen."

Her stomach clenched, the urgency in his tone making the hairs on the back of her neck rise. She had known this wasn't over. Arden's curse, the dark figures that stalked them, it was all connected—woven into something far darker than she had ever imagined. She had thought she was prepared to face whatever came next, but the raw fear in his eyes told her she was far from ready.

Evelyn's gaze darted around them, her pulse racing, but the shadows seemed to press in, suffocating everything in sight. She couldn't see them clearly—those who hunted them—but she could feel their presence like a creeping fog, something ancient and primal moving closer with each passing second. The trees around them creaked as if they, too, were holding their breath, waiting for what was to come.

"They're coming," Arden muttered, his voice taut with tension. "I don't know how much time we have."

Evelyn didn't have to ask who he meant. The figures in the woods—the ones that had been stalking them, moving closer every moment—were now within arm's reach, their shadows slithering between the trees like smoke, silent and swift. The growl of the leader echoed through the still air, a low, guttural sound that sent a shiver through her spine.

Then, out of the darkness, a figure stepped into view. Tall, with a long coat that fluttered in the wind, it moved with an unsettling grace. It wasn't human, not entirely—its skin seemed too pale, too smooth, as though it were made of something else, something not meant to exist. Its eyes gleamed in the dark, a dull gold that shone with an unnatural light. The air around it shimmered, like a heatwave rising from the earth, warping the edges of its form.

Evelyn's breath caught in her throat. She had seen creatures like this before, in passing—nightmares, myths whispered around campfires—but never up close. Never like this.

"Who are you?" Arden demanded, his voice a low growl, though there was no mistaking the underlying fear. "What do you want?"

The creature smiled—or, at least, something like a smile stretched across its face, sharp teeth glinting in the moonlight. "What do we want?" it echoed, its voice smooth like silk, but with an edge that cut through the night. "We want what's ours, of course. The silver mark is a prize, but the one who bears it is another matter entirely."

Evelyn's heart slammed against her ribs, her body stiffening at the words. The silver mark. The mark on Arden's skin. The very thing that had drawn them here. The thing that had tied them together in this dance of shadows and fear.

"Stay behind me," Arden muttered to her, his voice fierce, a protective edge cutting through his words. "Don't move."

But Evelyn didn't listen. The instinct to protect him was stronger than her fear, stronger than anything. She couldn't stay hidden, not while he faced whatever this thing was.

"I'm not hiding, Arden," she said, her voice firm, though it wavered under the weight of the terror pressing down on her. "You can't do this alone."

He turned to her then, his eyes flashing with something raw—desperation, anger, pain. "I don't want you involved in this, Evelyn," he snarled. "You don't understand what they'll do."

She stepped closer to him, defiance in her every movement, her heart pounding in her chest. "I don't care," she whispered, her voice soft but steady. "I'm here with you. Always."

The creature's eyes flicked to her, its lips curling into a twisted smile. "How touching," it said, its voice smooth and cruel. "But you are in far too deep, little girl. You don't know what you're dealing with."

Evelyn could feel Arden's hand at her back, pushing her gently but insistently, urging her to move away. But she refused to go. She couldn't leave him. Not now, when everything was falling apart.

"Don't," Arden muttered under his breath, his gaze flickering between her and the creature before him. His muscles were tense, his body prepared to strike. But the creature remained still, its unnatural stillness a threat all on its own.

The creature took a step forward, the ground beneath its feet shifting, the earth groaning in protest. "I can feel it, you know," it continued, its voice laced with venom. "The pull of the mark. The ancient power coursing through your veins. But it's not enough. Not yet."

Before Arden could react, the figure lunged, too fast for Evelyn to even register. She gasped, her heart lurching in her chest, but before she could scream, Arden was already moving—his body a blur of motion, his knife flashing in the dim light.

The creature's claws slashed through the air, but Arden was faster. He twisted, avoiding the attack with a fluid grace that belied the weight of his burden. He didn't pause, didn't hesitate, his every movement fueled by instinct and a desperate need to protect.

Evelyn's breath caught as the two figures clashed, the sound of metal meeting bone filling the air. Arden grunted, his face twisted in concentration, as he fought the creature off. But it was clear—the thing before him was stronger, faster, more relentless than anything they had faced before. The creature hissed, its claws grazing Arden's arm, and blood seeped from the wound.

Evelyn felt a wave of panic crash over her. She couldn't just stand there. Not when he was fighting for their lives. She reached for the dagger at her belt, her fingers trembling as she

The Ashen Encounter

drew it free. She might not be as skilled as Arden, but she wasn't about to be useless either.

As she moved forward, the creature's gaze shifted toward her, its smile widening. "A brave little thing," it purred, its voice like silk and poison. "But it won't save him. Nothing will."

Evelyn's heart raced, her legs nearly giving way under the weight of the moment. But then she felt it—a surge of power, strange and unfamiliar, coursing through her veins, as if the very blood in her body recognized the danger they were in. It was a momentary flicker of strength, something beyond her understanding, but it was enough.

She lunged.

The dagger felt foreign in her hand, but she gripped it tightly, her every muscle burning as she closed the gap between herself and the creature. She was going to do whatever it took to save Arden, even if it meant throwing herself into the fire.

But before she could strike, a sudden force slammed into her chest, throwing her backward. She gasped as the air rushed from her lungs, the ground hard beneath her as she crashed to the forest floor. Dazed, she struggled to breathe, her head spinning, but as her vision cleared, she saw Arden.

He was down, too.

The creature loomed over him, its eyes glowing with malice, and for a fleeting moment, Evelyn feared it was all over. They were too weak. Too far gone.

But then, something changed. Arden's hand shifted, his fingers brushing against the ground, and suddenly, his body was alight with a fierce, silvery glow, like the mark on his skin was burning through him from the inside.

The creature recoiled, its eyes widening in fear, but Arden wasn't finished.

He was just getting started.

Seven

The Choice of Silver and Ash

The forest had become a battlefield, a place where shadows warred against light, and the line between what was real and what was monstrous blurred into a twisted, inescapable haze. Evelyn stood at the edge of the clearing, her breath shallow, her fingers trembling against the cold hilt of the dagger she still held. The scent of earth and pine hung thick in the air, mingling with the metallic tang of blood, and the sounds of the forest were drowned out by the distant growls and snarls that echoed from the creatures that surrounded them.

Arden stood before her, his body still radiating the silvery glow. The light from the mark on his arm pulsed in rhythm with his heartbeat, each pulse sending ripples of energy through the air. He looked like a different person—stronger, more dangerous. But underneath it all, Evelyn could see the same man she had loved—the one who had once smiled so easily, who had held her hand with such quiet assurance.

But now, he was caught in something darker, something far older than they had imagined. Something that could break him, piece by piece.

"Arden," she breathed, her voice cracking as she took a step closer. Her heart pounded in her chest, the weight of everything that had happened pressing down on her. "What's happening? What is this power?"

He didn't turn to face her. His eyes were fixed on the creatures that circled them, the monsters from the darkness. His stance was rigid, his jaw clenched, and for the first time since he had returned to her, there was something in his eyes—something resigned. As if he had already made a decision, and it wasn't one she could change.

"The mark," he said, his voice hoarse, barely audible over the growls that filled the clearing. "It's not just a curse, Evelyn. It's… it's a tether. A binding. A promise made long ago by my ancestors."

Evelyn's stomach tightened. "A promise?" She couldn't help the incredulity that seeped into her words. What did that mean? What had his family gotten him involved in?

Arden's eyes flickered to her, his gaze briefly softening before hardening again, as if fighting the urge to pull her close and shield her from everything that was coming. "The mark connects me to something ancient, something powerful. Something that will stop at nothing to claim what's theirs."

"Stop?" Evelyn echoed, her pulse quickening. "You mean—" She couldn't finish the sentence. Her mind was still grappling with the enormity of what he was saying. The silver mark was a link to something not just ancient, but malevolent. She could see it in the way the creatures moved, the hunger in their eyes.

"Yes," he said, his voice trembling with what sounded like regret, but also resolve. "And it will consume me if I let it. If I let it pull me deeper into the darkness."

The creatures were closing in, circling them like wolves scenting fresh prey. Their eyes glowed a sickly yellow, their faces hidden in the shadows, but their bodies loomed large and powerful in the dim light. They were waiting for something—waiting for Arden to make his move.

Evelyn's heart raced, her instincts screaming at her to run, but her feet were rooted to the ground. She couldn't leave him. Not when he was so close to breaking.

"You don't have to face this alone," she said, stepping forward, her fingers brushing against his arm, the warmth of his skin comforting in contrast to the cold dread that was settling in her chest. She had always been the one to keep him grounded, to remind him of who he was before all of this darkness had taken over. But now, it was as if the world had shifted on its axis, and the person standing before her—her Arden—was a stranger wearing his face.

"I'm already too far gone, Evelyn," he whispered, his voice raw, as if the words themselves were tearing him apart. "There's a part of me that's not mine anymore. A part that belongs to them."

Her heart clenched. "No," she whispered fiercely. "You're still here. You're still with me. I won't let you go."

Arden's gaze flickered to her, his expression filled with something she couldn't quite read. Pain. Regret. And a trace of something darker, something that chilled her to her core. He reached for her, his hand trembling as it cupped her face, his thumb brushing the curve of her cheek.

"You don't understand," he whispered. "There are things I've done. Things that can't be undone. The power that the mark gives me—it's not just a gift. It's a chain."

Evelyn's breath hitched as his words settled into her chest, heavy and suffocating. She had always believed in the goodness of Arden, in the love they had shared, but now she could feel the weight of his past pressing against them both, dragging him further into the abyss. She didn't know what to do. How to save him from what had already claimed him.

But there was no time to dwell on that. The creatures were too close. Their growls were deafening now, the tension in the air thick and unbearable.

"We have to fight," Evelyn said, her voice firm, even though fear gnawed at her every word. She wasn't going to stand by and watch him fall. "I won't let them take you."

Arden didn't answer right away. His gaze turned inward, as though he was wrestling with something deeper than the threat before them. Then, finally, he spoke, his voice cold. "You don't understand, Evelyn. If we fight, there's no going back. They will destroy us. All of us."

The air around them felt heavy, as though the very atmosphere was reacting to his words, reacting to the decision that hung between them. Evelyn's heart pounded in her chest, her throat tight with emotion. She had come this far. She had fought so hard to bring him back from the edge, and now, it seemed like she was going to lose him again. But she couldn't—wouldn't—let that happen.

"I won't leave you," she said, her voice unwavering. "I'll face it with you. Whatever happens. We'll do this together."

Arden's hand fell from her face, and he looked away, his expression filled with a mix of sorrow and guilt. "I wish it were that simple," he said, almost to himself. "But the mark… it's not just a curse. It's a decision. A choice I made, long before I met you."

Evelyn felt the weight of his words like a cold hand on her chest. The truth was spilling out now, layer by layer, but it was too much to process all at once. Too much for her to understand.

Before she could respond, the creatures lunged. Their movements were blindingly fast, their eyes locked onto Arden, the power of the mark drawing them in like moths to a flame. But something inside her snapped. A rush of adrenaline, of instinct, surged through her veins. She didn't care if she didn't understand everything—she would fight. She would protect him, no matter the cost.

She moved, her body a blur as she struck, the dagger in her hand slicing through the air with precision. One of the creatures hissed in pain, its claws slashing toward her, but she was already gone, weaving through the shadows, focused entirely on the danger before them.

Arden, too, was moving now. The silver light from his mark blazed brighter than ever before, his body glowing with a power that seemed to emanate from the very core of him. He fought with a ferocity she had never seen, his every movement graceful, yet lethal. He was the man she loved, but also something more—something untouchable, something powerful.

The battle raged around them, but through it all, Evelyn's eyes never left Arden. The decision was clear. Whatever it took, she would stand by him. She would fight for him. And no matter what lay ahead, she would not let him face this alone.

Eight

Heart in the Flames

The air was thick with smoke, the scent of burning pine and ash curling around Evelyn as she stumbled through the dense forest. Her heart pounded in her chest, and each beat a frantic drum urging her to run and escape the flames that consumed the trees behind them. The crackling fire was a terrifying roar in the distance, but the silence of the world around them—the silence that had fallen over everything—terrified her most.

Arden was ahead of her, his silhouette cutting through the haze, his movements swift and deliberate as he led them through the chaos. The mark on his skin glowed brighter now, the silver light almost blinding as it illuminated the path before them. But even the light of the mark couldn't chase away the oppressive darkness that lingered just behind them. It was as if the very earth itself was trembling in the wake of the destruction, and Evelyn could feel it—could feel the power of the curse unraveling with every step they took.

She had no idea where they were going—had no idea how much longer they could outrun the terror that followed them. All she knew was that they couldn't stop. Not yet. Not when the fire was still chasing them, not when the shadows were still closing in.

"Evelyn!" Arden's voice broke through the haze, a sharp command that snapped her out of her spiraling thoughts. "Keep moving. Don't look back."

Her breath hitched in her throat, the weight of his words settling heavily on her chest. He didn't have to say it; she could feel the truth of it—the fire wasn't the only thing threatening them. It was the dark force that had been hunting them all along, that had been lurking just beneath the surface, waiting for the right moment to strike.

She nodded, pushing her body harder, her legs burning with exertion, but there was something else—something deeper that held her back. It wasn't just the fear of the creatures that had followed them. It was the feeling that something more dangerous was closing in. Something that wasn't just hunting them. Something that was waiting for them to make a mistake.

Evelyn's eyes flicked over her shoulder, searching for any sign of movement. The forest around them was still alive with the crackle of the fire, the trees silhouetted in a fiery glow, their leaves twisting in the smoke-heavy air. She saw nothing. Only the darkness, thick and oppressive, clinging to the edges of her vision. But even the darkness wasn't enough to shield them from what was coming. She could feel it. Could feel it in the tightening of her chest, in the breath that caught in her throat.

And then, she saw it.

A figure moved through the smoke, a shadow that slithered between the trees. It was fast, impossibly fast, and it was heading directly toward them.

"Arden!" she gasped, her voice tight with panic. "They're—"

She didn't have time to finish her sentence. The figure leapt from the shadows, a blur of motion and dark energy, and before she could react, it was upon them.

Arden's arm shot out, grabbing her by the wrist and yanking her out of harm's way. His body was a shield, his movements sharp and precise, but even he couldn't move fast enough to stop the creature from slashing toward them.

Evelyn's heart leaped into her throat as she watched the clawed hand reach for Arden. Time seemed to slow, the air thick with tension, and in that moment, she realized how close they were to the edge. The edge of everything. Of life. Of death.

But then, Arden moved.

He twisted, spinning on his heel with a speed that took Evelyn's breath away. His hand shot out, gripping the blade of his knife with a force that made it gleam in the moonlight, and in a single, fluid motion, he struck.

The creature's screech of pain was deafening. It recoiled, stumbling backward, its clawed hands swiping at the air as it howled. But it didn't retreat. No, it was only angrier now, more dangerous. It lunged again, its eyes glowing with an unholy light, and Evelyn's stomach churned as she saw the madness in its gaze.

Arden didn't hesitate. He was a blur of motion, his body moving with the precision of someone who had fought these creatures before. He ducked under the creature's swipe, his body low to the ground, and before it could react, he buried the blade in its side. The creature howled again, its body convulsing with the force of the blow. But Arden didn't stop. He twisted the knife, pulled it free, and plunged it back in.

Evelyn watched, her breath caught in her throat, as the creature staggered, its body writhing in agony. There was no mercy in Arden's eyes, no hesitation. He fought with the desperation of a man who had nothing left to lose.

But as the creature fell to the ground, its body crumpling like a puppet with its strings cut, Evelyn felt the air around them shift. It wasn't just the fire anymore. It was something else. Something more dangerous.

Arden stood, his body trembling with exhaustion, his breath coming in sharp, ragged gasps. The silver mark on his arm flickered, dimming for just a moment, before it flared back to life, brighter than before. He looked at her, his expression unreadable, his eyes dark with something she couldn't name.

"Are you alright?" he asked, his voice hoarse.

Evelyn nodded, though her heart was still racing in her chest. She was shaking, her hands trembling at her sides, but she couldn't let the fear take over. Not now. Not when there was still so much left to face.

"I'm fine," she whispered, though the words felt hollow in her mouth. "But this—this can't go on. We need to stop running."

Arden's gaze softened for a moment, and he stepped closer, his hand reaching out for hers. He took it, his touch warm and familiar, and for a brief moment, Evelyn thought she saw a flicker of the man he used to be. The man who had held her close and promised that they would always be together.

But then, his expression hardened, and the moment was gone.

"We don't have a choice, Evelyn," he said quietly, his voice filled with a sadness that made her heart ache. "This isn't something we can outrun. It's not something we can fight."

"What do you mean?" Her voice was barely a whisper, the question trembling on her lips. "What do you mean it's not something we can fight?"

Arden stepped back, his hand falling away from hers as he turned to face the fire that was now creeping toward them, its flames licking at the edges of the trees. The smoke was thick, suffocating, but it was the way the fire moved—ravenous, wild—that unsettled her. There was something unnatural about it.

He took a deep breath, his chest rising and falling with the weight of something unspoken. "The mark," he said slowly, his voice low and strained, "it's not just a curse, Evelyn. It's a call. A call to something much darker. The more we fight it, the stronger it gets."

Evelyn's heart sank. "So, what? We just give up?"

"No." Arden's voice was sharp, cutting through the night air. He turned to face her, his eyes meeting hers with a fierce intensity. "We don't give up. But the only way to stop this—stop the mark from consuming me—is to face it. To destroy it."

Evelyn's pulse quickened, and she took a step back, her mind racing with the implications of his words. "Destroy it? How?"

He didn't answer right away. Instead, he glanced over his shoulder at the fire, his face hardening.

"I don't know yet," he admitted quietly. "But whatever it takes, Evelyn. I'll do it. I'll do whatever it takes to save us."

The tension in the air was palpable, the weight of his words pressing down on her. They were standing on the edge of something. Something too big to ignore. And Evelyn knew, deep in her soul, that the choice they were facing would change everything.

And there would be no going back.

Nine

The Ritual of Blood and Ash

The clearing had fallen silent, save for the faint crackle of the fire behind them, its flames licking hungrily at the trees, casting long, twisted shadows across the ground. Evelyn's chest felt tight, her breath coming in shallow gasps as she stood at the edge of the circle, the air around her thick with the scent of smoke and something darker. The fire's heat was a distant thing, lost to the overwhelming presence of the ritual, the ancient force that hung in the air like an invisible weight.

Arden stood at the center of the circle, his posture rigid, his face set in a mask of determination. The silver mark on his arm blazed brightly, its light almost blinding as it pulsed with a rhythm of its own, beating in time with his heart. It was as though the very blood in his veins had become part of the curse, tied to something greater than the man she knew. And though she couldn't see it, Evelyn felt the darkness that lingered just beyond him, watching, waiting.

She swallowed hard, forcing her feet to move as she stepped closer, her fingers brushing the edge of the cold stone altar that stood before him. It was a relic, ancient and worn, its surface covered in strange symbols that seemed to shift when she wasn't looking directly at them. The air around it shimmered with an unnatural heat, and the longer she stood there, the more she felt the pull of it—like a tide drawing her into the depths of something she couldn't yet understand.

"Evelyn," Arden's voice was a low murmur, rough with emotion. "You don't have to do this. You don't have to be here."

She raised her eyes to meet his, her heart aching at the sight of him. He looked so different now, as if the very essence of who he was had shifted, twisted into something else entirely. The man she had loved—the man who had smiled at her with such tenderness—was now standing in the heart of a ritual he couldn't escape. The curse had consumed him, and now he was consumed by it.

"I'm not leaving you," she whispered, her voice trembling. "I can't."

He closed his eyes briefly, his jaw clenched as though fighting a battle within himself. "You don't understand. This… this is the only way. The only way I can break free from the curse." His voice was thick with guilt, his shoulders slumping under the weight of it. "I have to do this alone."

"No," she said firmly, stepping forward. Her feet felt heavy against the ground, as if the earth itself was trying to hold her back, to keep her from walking toward him. But she couldn't stop. She wouldn't. "You don't have to do this alone. I'm here with you. Always."

Her words hung between them, heavy with the promise she couldn't take back. She knew what he was facing—what they were both facing—but she couldn't bear to see him like this, standing on the precipice of something so dark, so dangerous, and so final.

Arden's eyes flickered to her, his gaze softening for just a moment before the mask of resolve slipped back into place. "You don't know what you're asking," he said quietly, his voice hoarse. "You don't know what it will cost."

"I don't care," Evelyn replied, her voice steady. "I'd rather face it with you than without you."

The words were out before she could stop them, and the weight of them settled into the air, thick and suffocating. There was no turning back now. She had already chosen her path, just as Arden had chosen his. Whatever happened next, they would face it together.

A tremor ran through the earth beneath their feet, subtle at first, but growing in intensity. The fire behind them roared louder, as if the flames themselves were responding to the ritual, feeding on the energy of the words they had spoken. The wind picked up, the sound of it whistling through the trees like a warning,

The Ritual of Blood and Ash

carrying with it the faintest echo of something ancient and forgotten.

"Are you ready?" Arden's voice was barely a whisper, but it carried through the chaos, steady and sure. There was no fear in his words, only the finality of someone who had already resigned himself to what was to come.

Evelyn nodded, her throat tight with unshed tears. She wasn't ready. No one could ever be ready for something like this. But she had no choice. She had already chosen.

The air shimmered, and the ground beneath them seemed to hum with an energy that made her skin prickle. A circle of light formed around Arden, bright and harsh, its edges flickering like flames, but it didn't burn. It was cold, unnervingly so, like the touch of death itself. And in that light, the symbols on the altar began to glow, shifting and rearranging as though they had a life of their own.

Evelyn's heart stuttered in her chest, her gaze flicking from Arden to the altar, the sense of wrongness growing with each passing second. She wanted to look away. She wanted to run, to tear herself from this place, but her feet were rooted to the ground. The air was too thick, too heavy, as if the ritual was pulling her into its web, trapping her here, in this moment, in this choice.

Arden took a step forward, his hand reaching toward the altar, his fingers brushing the cold stone. The moment his skin made contact, the ground trembled beneath them, and the fire behind them flared with an intensity that sent waves of heat crashing over her. But it was the sound—the sound that filled the air—that made her blood run cold. A deep, guttural voice that seemed to come from everywhere and nowhere, its words a language she couldn't understand.

"Blood is the price," the voice whispered, its tone as ancient as the earth itself. "Ash is the cost."

Evelyn's heart pounded in her chest, the words sinking deep into her bones. She didn't know what they meant, but she knew one thing for certain: they were more than just words. They were a promise. A curse.

The ground beneath them split open with a deafening crack, and a dark, swirling mist poured from the depths of the earth, coiling around Arden's feet like a serpent. It smelled of sulfur, of decay, and the very air seemed to vibrate with the power of it. Arden didn't flinch. He didn't even move. He was already part of this ritual, part of something greater than himself, something far older and far darker than the world she knew.

And then, the mark on his arm flared, brighter than ever before, its light cutting through the darkness like a blade. The wind howled around them, and for a moment, Evelyn thought she saw something move within the mist—something massive, something that could consume them both.

Arden's voice broke through the chaos. "This is the only way, Evelyn. The only way to break the curse. To end it."

She stepped forward, her hand reaching out toward him, her fingers brushing the edge of the circle of light. "I won't let you do this alone."

His eyes flickered to hers, and for a moment, the intensity in his gaze softened. There was love there, but there was also something darker—something she couldn't reach. The ritual was taking hold of him, and there was nothing she could do to stop it.

"I love you," he whispered, his voice ragged. "But this is something I must do. For us. For everything."

And then, with a single, final movement, he plunged his hand into the center of the altar. The mist roared around them, the fire behind them flaring once more, and the earth trembled beneath their feet.

Evelyn felt her heart stop in her chest, the world spinning around her as the very air grew thick with power, with heat, with ash. She wanted to scream, to tear herself away from the nightmare that was unfolding before her, but she couldn't. Not when the price of this ritual was already paid.

The choice had been made.

Ten

The Heart of the Storm

The storm raged around them, the winds howling like wolves at the gates of hell, tearing at the trees and whipping the flames into a frenzy. The sky above was a canvas of shifting black and silver, the clouds roiling with the weight of something ancient, something vast and unrelenting. Lightning crackled through the heavens, illuminating the landscape in brief flashes of violent light, casting long shadows that seemed to stretch across the earth like fingers reaching for something they could never touch.

Evelyn stood at the edge of the clearing, her body stiff with fear, her eyes locked onto Arden as he moved through the chaos. He was no longer the man she had known. The man she had loved. The ritual had changed him. The mark that had once been a symbol of his bloodline, of his family's pact with something darker, had consumed him, filling him with a power he could barely control. The light that pulsed from it was now blinding, flickering in time with his heartbeat, his chest rising and falling with each breath as though he were fighting against an invisible tide.

He wasn't the same. He wasn't himself.

And yet, he was still here. Still fighting.

"Arden," she whispered, her voice trembling with a mixture of awe and terror. She took a step forward, her heart hammering in her chest, but her feet felt heavy, as if the very ground was trying to hold her back. She couldn't explain it—couldn't understand what was happening—but she knew that the storm was more than just a physical one. There was something happening to Arden, something far deeper than the power of the mark, something that reached into the very core of him.

He turned to her then, his eyes wild with a fierce intensity, the silver light of the mark flickering in the depths of his gaze. For a moment, she saw the man she loved—the man who had held her, who had whispered promises into the night. But then it was gone, replaced by something darker, something she couldn't name. Something other.

"I told you to stay away," he growled, his voice strained, but there was a tremor in it now. It wasn't just the ritual's power; it was his power, too. It was beginning to break him.

"You don't get to tell me that," she shot back, her voice firm despite the panic that threatened to overwhelm her. "I'm not leaving you. Not now. Not when this—this is happening."

The wind screamed around them, drowning out her words, but she didn't need to say anything more. She could see the truth in his eyes. She could feel it. He was struggling—struggling against the curse, struggling against himself. The pull of the mark was too strong. She could see the tension in his body, the way his muscles clenched as though fighting an invisible force.

"I don't want this, Evelyn," he said, his voice raw with emotion. "But this power—it's too much for me. Too much for anyone. It will tear us apart if I don't stop it."

Her heart clenched, the words stabbing into her like a blade. She had known, deep down, that the path they were on wasn't going to end easily. But she hadn't realized just how far it had gone. He wasn't just fighting for survival anymore. He was fighting for his very soul.

"No," she said, her voice trembling but unwavering. "You're not alone in this. I'll fight with you, Arden. I won't let you go."

He shook his head, his eyes flickering with a painful mixture of love and desperation. "You don't understand. There is no choice left. The only way for me to survive this… is to destroy what remains of me."

A cold shiver ran down her spine, and her pulse quickened, the truth of his words sinking in like a stone. She could see it now—the destruction that was already unfolding inside him. The mark was pulling him toward something dark, something that would consume everything in its wake.

The storm grew fiercer, the winds whipping around them with a violent energy, and Evelyn felt a knot form in her stomach. This was no ordinary storm. The air crackled with an otherworldly power, thick and suffocating, as if the very heavens were responding to the ritual's power. The ground beneath their feet trembled, and the earth groaned in protest, as though the world itself was fighting to hold on.

Evelyn stepped forward, closer to Arden, ignoring the way her heart was racing in her chest. The raw emotion she saw in his eyes—torn between love and desperation—was more than she could bear. He was slipping away, piece by piece, and there was nothing she could do to stop it. The curse had already claimed him. And she wasn't sure if there was any part of him left that she could reach.

But she wasn't giving up. She couldn't.

"Arden," she whispered again, taking his hand in hers. His skin was burning, as if the fire within him was alive, and she could feel the heat of it seeping into her own bones. She looked up at him, her voice steady despite the fear that threatened to choke her. "I love you. Whatever happens, I'm here. I'll be here, no matter what."

For a long moment, Arden didn't respond. His eyes searched hers, flickering with something that could have been guilt, or sorrow, or something darker. But then he closed his eyes, as though surrendering to whatever was inside him, and a tear slipped down his cheek.

"I don't want to hurt you," he whispered, his voice breaking. "But I don't know if I can stop it. I don't know if I can stop myself."

Evelyn's chest tightened with the weight of his words, the weight of everything they had lost—and everything they still stood to lose. But she couldn't walk away from him now. Not after everything they had been through, not after the promise they had made to each other so long ago. He was still Arden, still the man who had held her heart, and she wasn't going to let the curse take him.

The wind howled around them, the trees creaking and groaning as if they, too, were caught in the chaos of the ritual. Lightning flashed overhead, casting the clearing in an eerie, almost ghostly light. The power in the air was palpable now, filling her senses, drowning out everything else. The ground trembled beneath her feet, and the sound of the storm intensified, as though it were reaching its crescendo.

Arden's breath was shallow, his chest heaving with the effort to control the rising tide of the mark. He looked at her, his gaze filled with an intensity that cut through her, and for a fleeting moment, she saw the man she had fallen in love with—the man who had promised her forever. And in that moment, she made her decision.

"Arden," she said again, her voice steady now, her eyes never leaving his. "We'll find a way through this. Together. You don't have to fight alone."

His eyes flickered, uncertainty flashing across his face, but it was gone as quickly as it had appeared. He clenched his jaw, his body trembling with the effort to hold on to what was left of himself, and Evelyn could see it—the battle he was fighting inside, the fight to keep himself from surrendering completely to the curse.

For a moment, time seemed to slow, the storm, the ritual, everything around them fading into the background as they stood together, locked in that one, single moment. And then, slowly, with a movement that seemed to take every ounce of strength he had left, Arden stepped forward, his arms wrapping around her, pulling her close.

"I'm sorry," he whispered into her hair, his voice a soft, broken murmur. "I'm sorry for everything."

Evelyn's heart ached as she pressed her cheek to his chest, feeling the steady beat of his heart beneath her ear, as though it was the only thing keeping them both anchored to the world. "No," she whispered, her voice full of love and conviction. "You don't have to be sorry. I'm here. We're here."

And for a brief moment, in the eye of the storm, they stood together—two souls bound by love, by fate, and by the dark forces that threatened to tear them apart. But Evelyn knew, deep in her heart, that no matter what happened next, she would never stop fighting for him.

Not now. Not ever.

Eleven

Into the Ashes

The fire was a beast now. It had grown, no longer merely a threat to the forest but to everything around it. The flames were wild, uncontrollable, hungrily devouring anything in their path, the heat so intense that the air itself shimmered and warped. Evelyn stood in the clearing, her eyes fixed on Arden as he moved toward the fire, his figure bathed in the orange glow of the flames. His silver-marked arm flickered like a beacon in the chaos, a stark contrast to the inferno that surrounded them.

The storm had stopped. The winds had died down, leaving only the crackling fire and the strange, suffocating stillness that had descended upon the world. The trees creaked and groaned, their branches heavy with the weight of the fire's rage, and the earth itself seemed to hum with the power of the ritual. It was as if the world had held its breath, waiting for what was to come next.

Evelyn's heart hammered in her chest. She had no idea what Arden was doing, no idea how close he was to completing the ritual—or destroying them both—but she knew one thing with a certainty that felt like a knife lodged in her throat: He was slipping away from her.

His movements were slow now, deliberate, his body shaking with the effort to keep himself grounded. The mark on his arm pulsed, casting eerie shadows across his face, and his expression was one of agony. His breath was shallow, each inhale a laborious effort as if the curse was tightening its grip on him. But there was something else—something darker—that she couldn't ignore. It wasn't just the ritual that was pulling him. It was himself, fighting against something inside, fighting against the very thing that had made him who he was.

"Arden..." She whispered his name, but it was lost in the roar of the fire. She couldn't bear to watch him like this. She couldn't bear to see him torn apart by the very thing that had bound them together.

He didn't respond, didn't turn to face her. His focus was entirely on the fire, on the altar that stood just beyond the flames, a dark presence in the heart of the storm. The ancient symbols carved into the stone altar glowed with the same sickly light that now radiated from his mark. The flames seemed to recognize the altar, dancing and flickering with a strange reverence.

Evelyn's feet moved before her mind could catch up. She had

to get to him. She had to stop him before it was too late. The ritual was already in motion, but there was a part of her—an irrational part—that still clung to the hope that they could stop it. That they could stop him from making the ultimate sacrifice.

But as she stepped closer, the ground beneath her feet trembled. The fire surged forward, as if it had become a living thing, trying to push her away, trying to protect the ritual. Evelyn stopped dead in her tracks, her heart racing as the heat washed over her. The flames were now a living wall between her and Arden, their heat so intense that she could feel the burn on her skin even from this distance.

She could see him now, standing just beyond the fire, his body stiff with the strain of whatever was happening inside him. His breath came in sharp, ragged gasps, and his fingers clenched into fists at his sides. She could feel the pain emanating from him, like an invisible force pressing down on her chest, making it harder to breathe. The love she had for him was still there, raw and unyielding, but it was tangled with something darker now—something she couldn't fully grasp.

"Arden!" she called out, her voice sharp with desperation. "Don't do this!"

For a moment, it seemed as if he didn't hear her. His gaze remained fixed on the altar, on the energy that seemed to pulse from it, like a heartbeat echoing through the air. The mark on his arm flared once more, blindingly bright, and Evelyn had to squint against the light.

And then, he looked at her.

His eyes met hers, and for a brief moment, she saw him—the man she had known, the man she had loved. But the moment was fleeting, gone before she could hold onto it. His gaze darkened, and his expression shifted, hardening into something cold, something distant.

"It's too late for me, Evelyn," he said, his voice hoarse, barely audible over the crackle of the fire. "This is the only way. The only way I can stop it."

"No." Her voice broke, the word a plea, a desperate cry to stop him from sacrificing himself. "Please don't say that. There's always a way out, Arden. I'll find it."

His gaze softened, just for a moment, but then the fire flared again, and the light in his eyes flickered. "You can't save me," he said softly, his voice filled with a bitter sadness. "You can't save me from what's inside."

Evelyn's heart clenched in her chest. "I don't care what's inside you. I care about you," she said fiercely, her feet moving again despite the heat that was now unbearable. "Whatever this is, whatever has happened to you, I won't lose you. Not to this. Not to them."

The fire surged, as if to drown out her words, the flames licking higher into the sky, casting long, jagged shadows across the ground. But she wouldn't stop. She couldn't.

Evelyn pushed forward, her body heat-ravaged and her chest burning with the force of her emotions. She had to get to him, had to make him understand. They weren't just fighting against the curse now; they were fighting against the very thing that had driven them apart.

"Arden!" she screamed, her voice raw with desperation. "Please. You don't have to do this alone."

And then, with a sudden movement, Arden broke. His body tensed, the muscles in his arms straining as if something inside him had snapped. His hand reached for the altar again, his fingers trembling as they brushed against the stone. The mark on his arm blazed brighter, so bright that Evelyn had to shield her eyes. The ground beneath them groaned, the earth shaking as if in response to his touch.

"No…" she whispered, her voice catching in her throat.

The air around them shimmered, the world warping in strange, unnatural ways. The wind howled again, whipping around them with such force that it felt as though the very atmosphere was alive, closing in on them.

And then, suddenly, everything stopped.

The world went silent. The fire froze in place, its flames still and unmoving, casting long, eerie shadows that seemed to stretch endlessly into the night. The wind stilled, and the air grew thick, the tension so heavy that it felt as though time itself had stopped.

Evelyn's breath came in shallow gasps as she stood frozen in place, her eyes locked on Arden. His body was still, but the power in the air—surging, wild, untamed—was palpable. She felt it wash over her, felt it reaching for something deep inside her, pulling at the very core of her being.

The silver mark on Arden's arm began to pulse again, slowly at first, then faster, as if responding to an unseen force. It was almost as if the mark had a life of its own now, growing, feeding, and consuming everything around it. Evelyn's heart raced in her chest as the light grew, brighter and brighter until it was blinding, until she couldn't see anything but the light and the shadow it cast.

And then, the mark exploded.

A blinding flash of silver and light burst from Arden's arm, washing over everything in a wave so powerful that Evelyn was thrown back, her body slamming into the ground as the world around her shattered into pieces. She could feel the heat of the explosion, the power of it reverberating through her, shaking her to the core.

The light, the power, it all consumed her.

And then, silence.

Twelve

Heart Reborn

~~~~~~

The silence was suffocating.

Evelyn's chest ached with the absence of sound, the kind of silence that had settled in after a storm—unnatural, thick, and cold. She lay on the ground, her body aching, her skin scorched by the force of the blast, her hair damp with the sweat of fear and exertion. Her pulse hammered in her ears, and yet, there was no sound from the world around her. The fire had stopped its roar, the wind its furious howling. Even the trees stood still, as though they, too, were holding their breath.

She blinked, her vision blurry from the blinding light of the explosion that had sent her crashing to the earth. The taste of ash was thick in her mouth, and she felt the remnants of the heat cling to her skin like a second layer of fire. But the sting of her injuries—both physical and emotional—couldn't overpower the suffocating sense of dread that gripped her heart.

Where was Arden?

The world seemed frozen in time. She pushed herself up from the dirt, her limbs heavy, her head spinning with the force of everything that had just happened. She could still feel the pulse of power that had surged through the air, but it felt distant now, a lingering presence rather than a tangible force. The silver mark on Arden's arm had erupted in a blaze that had felt like the unraveling of something ancient, something irreversible.

She didn't understand what had happened. She didn't know what the explosion had meant, but she knew one thing: she had to find him.

"Evelyn?"

Her name. His voice. It sliced through the silence like a knife, and she turned, almost instinctively, her heart leaping in her chest.

Arden was standing a few feet away, his back to her, his body bathed in the faint light of the fading fire. But he wasn't the same. Not at all.

The silver mark on his arm was gone.

It had vanished completely, leaving behind nothing but pale skin where once the glowing, pulsating symbol had been. His body was still trembling, his form hunched as though he was struggling to hold himself together. His dark hair was matted against his forehead, sweat and dirt streaking his face, but his eyes—those eyes—were still the same. Still filled with that same warmth that had always been there, no matter the darkness he had carried inside him.

Evelyn's breath caught in her throat. "Arden…" She stood slowly, her legs unsteady as she took a hesitant step toward him. Her heart was hammering in her chest, but this time, it wasn't from fear. It was from the rush of hope that surged through her, strong and dangerous.

He turned to face her, his movements slow, as though he were still getting used to his own body. His eyes locked onto hers, and for the first time in what felt like forever, the weight of the curse seemed to lift from him. He was still there. He was still Arden.

But there was something else in his gaze. Something she couldn't quite place. The love she had seen before—the love that had always anchored them—was still there, but there was also a quiet sadness, an emptiness that seemed to stretch between them.

"Evelyn," he repeated, his voice hoarse, almost broken. "I didn't think… I didn't think I'd ever see you again."

Her heart skipped a beat. She wanted to rush toward him, to pull him into her arms, to feel the heat of his body against hers, but she hesitated, unsure. She didn't know what had happened to him. She didn't know what the ritual had done.

"What did you do?" she whispered, her voice barely a breath. "The mark—where did it go?"

Arden's gaze flickered to his arm, the place where the silver mark had been. He touched the skin there gently, almost as if checking to see if it was real. "It's gone," he said softly, his voice filled with awe and something else—something darker. "It's over."

Evelyn's chest tightened. Over. What did that mean? Had he succeeded in breaking the curse, or had he paid an even greater price than she'd realized? Was he truly free?

Before she could ask, he took a step toward her, his eyes still locked on hers. His presence was overwhelming, his energy now shifting, a quiet storm that pulled her in, drew her closer. And yet, she could still feel the distance between them, the gap that had widened after everything they had been through—the betrayal of the curse, the ritual that had torn him apart, and the fear that still lingered in her chest.

"I'm sorry," he said suddenly, his voice thick with emotion. "I never wanted to drag you into this. Into my mess."

Evelyn shook her head, her heart aching. She moved toward him, her legs unsteady, but she didn't care. She couldn't stop herself. The pull between them was undeniable. "You didn't drag me into anything, Arden. I chose this. I chose you."

For a moment, Arden didn't speak. His eyes softened, the pain in them raw and exposed, and for the first time since he had stepped into the ritual, he seemed human again. He seemed real.

"I never wanted you to see this side of me," he whispered, his voice almost breaking. "I never wanted you to know the darkness I carry. The things I've done, the things I've become."

Evelyn's heart squeezed in her chest. She took another step forward, her hands trembling as she reached for him. "Arden, listen to me. I know what you've been through. I know the curse has been tearing you apart, but you're still here. You're still you. That's all that matters."

The words spilled out before she could stop them, her emotions rushing forward like a flood. She had seen him at his worst. She had seen him struggle, lost in the power of the curse, a slave to something that had threatened to swallow him whole. And yet, here he was, standing before her, free of it. Free.

His breath caught as she reached for him, her fingers brushing against his cheek, and for the first time, she felt the warmth of him—the warmth that had once been the anchor to her world. She could feel the faint thrum of his pulse beneath her touch, the steady rhythm of it, like a lifeline.

"I'm here, Arden. I'm right here." Her voice was soft, almost a whisper, but it carried with it all the things she couldn't say in words. The fear, the love, the longing.

Arden closed his eyes for a moment, and when he opened them again, the darkness that had once clouded them seemed to have lifted. There was something softer in his gaze now, something that hadn't been there before. He looked at her, his expression filled with tenderness, but also with something else. A lingering doubt.

"I don't deserve you," he said quietly, his voice barely a whisper. "After everything... after what I've done, I don't deserve you."

"Stop," she said firmly, her voice steady despite the flutter in her chest. "You don't get to say that. You've been through enough. And you're here. With me. That's all that matters."

Arden's breath hitched, and his hand moved to cover hers, his touch warm and grounding. For a long moment, neither of them spoke, as if the weight of everything they had been through needed to settle before they could go on.

And then, slowly, almost imperceptibly, Arden leaned forward, his lips brushing against her forehead in a soft, tender kiss. It was gentle, almost reverent, like he was afraid to break something, to shatter the fragile peace that had settled between them.

"I'm sorry," he whispered again, his lips still close to her skin. "For everything. For making you part of this... mess."

Evelyn smiled softly, her eyes fluttering closed as she leaned into him. "We've both been in this together, Arden. Always. We're not done yet."

And as she held him, as she felt his arms wrap around her, the world around them seemed to exhale. The fire was now only a distant crackle, the smoke thick in the air, but for a brief moment, there was peace. No more curses. No more battles. Just the two of them, standing in the quiet aftermath of a storm that had threatened to destroy them.

For the first time in what felt like forever, Evelyn felt the weight of the world lift, and for the first time, she allowed herself to hope. Because maybe, just maybe, they could rebuild. Together.

www.ingramcontent.com/pod-product-compliance
Lightning Source LLC
LaVergne TN
LVHW010602070526
838199LV00063BA/5046